Journey to the Corrida

Books by Donald Junkins

The Sunfish and the Partridge
The Graves of Scotland Parish
Walden, 100 Years After Thoreau
And Sandpipers She Said
The Uncle Harry Poems
The Contemporary World Poets (anthology)
The Agamenticus Poems
Crossing by Ferry: poems new and selected
Playing For Keeps

Journey to the Corrida

Poems

Donald Junkins

Lynx House Press

Portland, Oregon ❖ *Spokane, Washington*

Design by Christine Holbert

First Edition

Library of Congress Catalogue in Publication Data

Junkins, Donald, 1931.
Journey to the Corrida : poems / by Donald Junkins
p.   cm.
ISBN 0-89924-100-X (paper)
1. Bullfights – Poetry.
I. Title.
PS3560.U6J86 2000
811' .54 – dc21

Lynx House Press books are distributed by

Small Press Distribution
1341 Seventh Street
Berkeley, CA 94710
or
Lynx House Press
9305 SE Salmon Court
Portland, OR 97216
or
Lynx House Press
420 West 24 Street
Spokane, WA 99203

Acknowledgements

Some of the poems in this collection appeared previously in the following journals:

America
La Busca
The Cincinnati Review
Colorado North Review
Field
The Greensboro Review
Journal of the Club Taurino of New York
The North Dakota Quarterly
Las Noticias Pena Taurina Sol Y Sombra
Prairie Scooner
Salmagundi.

Table Of Contents

I

II

III

No single word in English accurately describes the meaning of the Spanish word "corrida" : literally, "the running of the bulls." The English word "bullfight" does not communicate the ritual and mystic tragedy of *toreo* which has focused a significant element of Spanish culture since the 16th century. Garcia Lorca said, "Spain is the only country where death is the national spectacle, where death sounds long trumpets at the arrival of springtime. The only serious thing left in the world is *toreo*. *Tore* is the liturgy of the bulls, an authentic religious drama where, just as in the Mass, there is the adoration and sacrifice of a God." The idea of "fight" is wrong. (If there were a fight, the bull would always win.) Instead there is a ritual sacrifice of the totemic animal whose tragedy is played out in the spectacle.[1]

[1] The statement by Lorca is quoted in Sandra Forman and Allen Josephs, ONLY MYSTERY: GARCIA LORCA'S POETRY IN WORD AND IMAGE, University Press of Florida, 1992, p. 95.

Glossary of Terms and References

1. "Behold, there was a swarm of bees and honey in the carcass of the lion": Judges 15: 8
2. *Chinampas:* a town in the province of Jalisco, Mexico.
3. *El Yiyo:* the Spanish matador who was on the cartel with Paquirri when he was fatally gored, and who killed Paquirri's bull, by law: a year later *Yiyo* himself was killed.
4. *Formazza:* a narrow geographical area in northern Italy above Domodossola which extends into the Swiss Alps.
5. *Ganaderia:* a ranch where fighting bulls are raised.
6. *Indian Camp:* the site near Walloon Lake in northern Michigan of a short story of that title by Ernest Hemingway.
7. *Jeu De Boule:* A French game, sometimes called *petanque,* in which the players throw heavy steel balls as close as possible to a randomly tossed anchor object twenty to thirty feet away.
8. *Ponte san Giovanni: a* town near Perugia in Umbria, Italy.
9. *Pozoblanco:* a small town in the province of Cordoba in southern Spain where Paquirri was fatally gored.
10. *Recibiendo:* a form of killing the bull in which the matador receives the charge of the bull without moving his feet once the bull has started for him. The rarest and most dangerous, therefore emotional, way to kill a bull.
11. *Tienta:* a bull breeding event at a *ganaderia* where male and female calves are tested for bravery.
12. *toro:* fighting bull.
13. *muleta:* scarlet cloth draped over a wooden stick, used to perform a series of passes with the bull.

For Scott Schereschewski

I

"On the rough wet grass of the back yard my father and mother have spread quilts. We lie there, my mother, my father, my uncle, my aunt, and I too am lying there. First we were sitting up, then one of us lay down, and then we all lay down, on our stomachs, or on our sides, or on our backs, and they kept on talking."

— *James Agee*

"And so I learned that familiar paths traced in the dusk of summer evenings may lead as well to prisons as to innocent, uncontrolled sleep."

— *Meursault in* THE STRANGER
by Albert Camus

BEFORE DAWN THEY HEAR THE AUTUMN RAIN

And he touches her. Hear it?
It's Spain somewhere, she says:
the wet leaves, the sparrows of Lazarus.

LINES BEGUN NEAR THE SHORE IN A HIGH WIND

The low roof pot swings
empty over the dark deck; two blue
flags snap-flutter on grommet rings
down the driftwood mast. "Who

are you dear?" my mother asked
last summer, eating her apple, her wig
awry under the sweeping gull's eye, basking
sweater-cozy in the sun. I was rigging

the extension ladder to stain the topmost
cedar shakes. "You mean *I* bore
you?" — and struck the driftwood railing post
laughing, nibbling her apple core

to the seeds. She dozed in the August
heat. I dabbed and brushed the dark
oil in as the breeze wavered in cooling gusts
off the water. In her sleep she mumbled "Hark,

hark." Later she said "You mustn't mind me, dear,
but where have I been all these years?"
Now the island weather has changed again.
The blue flags drape, and the fog is rolling in.

THE NIGHT ISLAND WIND

A big-eared mouse appears
and disappears behind the corner
boot, hearing

no footfall, no heavy-handed
log topping the birch-sogged
flames. Dead

soot crisps and drops into the fall's
first fireplace glow. All
summer I followed

her tracks with an owner's scorn
for untidy guests horning
in. Now shorn

of the easy confidence that comes
lying alone in the August sun,
pastor John,

I am undone in my own house.
I hear the high tide roar as the mouse
carefully browses

in the tinkling pans. Without wit
I brought Joan the deadly news at lunch, the tidbit
that hurts,

and headed out on the ferry's leisurely run
to the oiled deck cold with beach stones,
pine cones

piled for the autumn fire. Wee
beastie, Burns called you, and me,
listen; the sea

roars exactly as the half-moon
rises over the yodel of the gone
summer loon.

PAINTING THE FRONT BOW WINDOW

The yellow locust tree butters
the grass of this closeup
view: necklace arms fluttering.

*My mother fixes the white lace
on my yellow blouse; my first day
in the second grade. I see her face.*

I brush each brown panel white.
The second coat does the trick. Beech
leaves drift against the white

mums. *Marjorie Blood holds a buttercup
under my chin in Wormstead's field. Do you
like butter? Do you? Yup.*

Oyster mushrooms clump in the second maple
stump. *At the farm my mother
says my gosh you're handsome. Tell*

*me something, are you my younger
brother?* There are twelve sills
to brush. *I tell her*

yes. Traces of brown stain bleed
in this gloss. The blue sky frames
that squirrel in the red oak, two acorn seeds

bulge his cheeks. I rap the pane
and his eyes blaze. Hush,
hush: the brush moves over the sash and the grain

disappears for now. These versions
carry over in the short run. *Last week
we lay on the mountain in the sun.*

It's not you, you said, it's me.
The whole valley was neckcurls
and a river softening south. We

walked later beyond the Sunderland town
park. Close up again, the clear pane
brightens the honey locusts and the tiger's frown.

I see them as clear as that child in the front room:
the yellow leaves in their final flutter;
the tigers circling in their meltdown into butter.

DRIVING TO SCHOOL, THE ENGLISH TEACHER

plays the station with the song
that stings, switches
to Berlioz on the tape deck *(words
are only sounds that sound like words)*.
She worries the pedal at the light, switches
back *(at least I have the song)*.

Driving to school, the English teacher plays
with words: wonders
if Eleanor will show today, or ever; if
James will be sober in the Beowulf class; if
Hunt will turn on in the teacher's room. She wonders
where she'll be in June, if she'll play

out the song. Driving, the English teacher
runs over the words, drives
the landscape of her mind.
The song insists. She doesn't want to mind
it when she gets this far *(drive,
drive)*. The English teacher

plays the station with the song
that turns her down, switches
to Mozart, drives in cruise control *(words
have always done me in, words
will always do me)*. On the final hill she switches
out of cruise, the car riding like a song.

the spring rain surrounds the phone
call, and the dial tone after
our reading in the Philadelphia
park, the first chapter

of the garden, the blue
wedding party from the new
cars, stepping past us on the grass
in silence to the tiny wine glass

island where the boy threw bread
flopping his net too late and you said
it's an Antonini movie and no one else will see
us in the picture until we

enlarge it for them years from now
and all the bright colors fade to show
our truest image on the bamboo mat:
your chin on your hands flat

over your knees, the silent blue
dresses in your eyes as he tires the fish to
the bank, the waiter saying *softly now*
softly for us all before the boy asks how

to make the net work and the springer
leave his bread alone and the water
shallower so he can get across to the good
place and the chapter ends *good-*

bye my lovely girl and good luck and goodbye
and we fold the bamboo under the bright spring sky
shouldering the boy to the island one jump
away, our bargain kept, our hearts pumping

even and true from the park
and beyond, the two lucky pennies in the dark
folds of your leather boots rhyming
in silence in your pacing, in your timing.

OPENING DEREK WALCOTT'S SEA GRAPES

I find your last spring's note:
your blue-inked rag paper
card, hoping my day's
been mine. You are so tired
you can hardly see straight but may swim
at four. If so, you'll be home

at half-past five: *Hang tight.*
I read some lines here in the Deerfield
woods while snow melts
from my roof. Below me a gray squirrel
raids the suction feeder on my kitchen
window, bold as damned Billy, squat

in the cookie seeds, brandy-eyed. In
the scope of my .22 his gray tail
feathers a switch. I close Walcott's "Love
after Love," replace SEA GRAPES
on the shelf. Between the lines
you are overhanding the fast lane

like sixty.

A DREAM OF GIRAFFES

Waking in mid-afternoon, she smooths
the bent pages of her fallen
book: slowly laces her running
shoes. On the road, a fallen
ash marks the late storm, smooths
the Berkshire laurel running

wild. She slows her pace
to slow down time: you *may*
take, you may stay, the old voices
say. Her breathing says *I may,*
I may. She lets the voices
go. She takes the landscape at her pace:

embossed barns in an ample space
where loss is exact. Imagined scrubs
are going by. She runs her way:
Monterey (Massachusetts) to real scrub
oaks in line for breathing space;
she runs all the way

home and back, and home, running
awkward easy among the leaves
head high, her skin soft
in the autumn sun, eyes of leaves
gauging the falling of her soft
steps, her lost days, her minutes running.

THAT AFTERNOON BY THE FEATHER RIVER

she edged across the bog-clefts
and spotted him downstream casting
for rainbows. Spotted blue dress, casting
the ladybug hatch in its own clefts

of light, the red dream rippling its seams
she ran to the cabin's loft, her mother's
ladybug-keeping in a mother's
ladybug sleep. She knew then, or so it seems.

NOW THAT IT'S APRIL

I sleep in the corner room downstairs
on the southeast side of the house
overlooking the white sub of pyrofax gas
in the woods and the clothesline fancy with yesterday's
wash

over the spring brook that baubled
when I was hanging it but now settles
in pools seeping around the plaited levelings
descending toward the swamp below. As the pools

expose their rock garden slates each year
I haul them to my iris beds and the forsythia
knoll bright with my mother's lost ideas
of color not my own. Further in the woods, mayflowers

are doing what they do. She used to say
"April showers bring May flowers" in a way
that made me think the blossoms would appear in May.
Next Sunday is Mother's Day

and her abandoned garden is all around
me in this room. I woke to the robin
thumping against the cellar window
mistaking her orange image, burdened

in the sunrise sun. Now I doze among portraits
on my blue and yellow walls, faces waiting
in the season's hush, my own, my son,
a lady in long hands and a blue gown

(a *dessin* from Paris by Jaqueline Oblin),
and Vermeer's girl with the blue turban
and the brown eyes, her lips barely open
in her pleasant quizzical gaze. All our heads are turned

toward a certain kind of light. Outside,
a lone long arm of forsythia lopes
out of my transplant, dangling over moss clawed
by my spring rake, groping

DEEP JUNE ONSHORE, OPENING UP

The wind rushes the poplars, and the wild rose
ruffles by the rotting deck. I cannot see
Ram Island for the larch arms now between me
and old news. Whose death tolls

off Sunken Money Ledge? I have cut
a thousand branches to keep the lower
view. Earlier, two kayaks and their paddlers
gleamed from Red Point to the Sister Island's hut.

Here my deck chair frays. The railing-mast
from the Muscongus Bay sloop floats
between deck posts, punky: my daughter's seven coats
of yellowed varnish peels. The past

is something else again. When I was a child
I found a Collier's magazine in a gold mine camp
above Lynn Bay, Alaska, Eddie Cantor
ogling on the cover, asking calmly wild-eyed,

"Will America ever be rich again?" Last night
at dusk I untied the nylon knot on the bleached-pole
nail and raised the Big Dipper toward the black hole
in the sky. Now in the morning light

the blue flag flutters against the spruce dark green
toward the open sea. Off in the woods a mourning dove
knits and pearls. I cannot measure the silence of this cove
as the noon tide comes in. Overhead a single gull careens.

LOOKING SOUTH

Fishing yachts cream the cutting edge
of this turquoise mirage

and summer slows to your letters and the dolor
of sails off the beach; color

them green, yellow, red, sky blue, all
Dufy; white clouds small

in the distance looming, coming
to nothing overhead, days apart from you honing

in. Last night a jeweler showed me
two strands of lapis lazuli

and pearls, pure nacre and Chinese blue
for your healing ears, a double view

of global things,
earrings

of this summer sky and the distant amethyst
Gulf Stream, you here in Key West.

SUNDAY MORNING

Veins of palm fronds brush above the shore
in the high-tide breeze, feigning restlessness
and a guardian pause, our whispers of *more*,
more postponed in the languor
of proffered arms on quaint side streets, *yes*
to the tropic goddess:
warm air off the water.
Soft. Hear

these spine-yellow, greenfan
Venetians
as they pose: storkish, androgynous, teeming
with belly nuts, fawning
over the tropical fair
of curved orange-billed ibises, shell lairs
of hermits walking their aquamarine
zones. Waves wash their feet in erogenous tones.

AFTERNOON SHADOWS THE STALKING HERONS

in low-tide lakes of glass:
black profiles occasionally gash

up to meet the white gleams
flashing down

to nail the crab
in a pinpoint grab.

The herons wait,
deliberate

toward ocean space,
mirroring themselves in gawky grace

to us who watch, profiling our own
shadowy passion

for the waiting game.
Timing, again and again they poise over the same

submerged clue
deliberately un-disturbed, brand new.

We spend years formalizing
the mere recognition of the thing

that moves and draws us irresistibly,
salty,

to our mouths. Savoring,
pondering,

we gaze toward the azure stillness
of the distant Stream

deeper than the shadows shadowing us
in this crabgrass lake far from home.

SUNDAY RAIN

rolls like mercury off the nasturtium leaves,
Asian flathats bowing
at the end of summer. We drank tea here
in June before the green veins

leveled between the geranium
and the chrysanthemum reds.
Now water bevels, forms nod,
clearing the green pads

for balance. The tone is delicate
heady, but ritual belies timing
in green hearts holding dear
their weight, then letting go

(in July I saw the impassioned bull
drop the gored *pastor* to the sand
and canter to the pen). Form
shifts with its own weight,

holding us alone, mercurial.

II

"Jesus said to them, 'When you make the two one, and when you make the inside like the outside and the outside like the inside, and the above like the below, and when you make the male and the female one and the same, so that the male not be male nor the female female; and when you fashion eyes in place of an eye, and a hand in place of a hand, and a foot in place of a foot, and a likeness in place of a likeness, then will you enter the Kingdom.'"

The Gospel of Thomas (ii, 2)
The Nag Hammadi Library

IT BEGINS WITH THE SWALLOWS

over Mijas, glide-diving
the pool, your exquisite-gawky
gait;

unraveling
above the Mediterranean
in late June of the high

winds;
        you want to see
the *corrida*, the black
ribbon-backed charge to the cape

draped later over the sword, over
the needle eye, the plunge
after the surface nicking

after the ring talk, the *toro*
talk. Bulls charging. Swallows
drinking.

OLEANDER

Red oleander blazes
so precisely in the mountain crabgrass lawns
facing the Mediterranean haze
that imprecisions calm

our summer days: the way
water forms on our thigh
under our book in the sun, and dries
when we raise it to brush at the fly;

the way swallows cloud,
sweep across the pool and disappear
in arrays of whiteblue vests, wing shrouds
into the blue, pepper

over the haze; even the way
we parcel to ourselves our random
versions of that summer galley
easing toward open

ocean, rust-brown as these
fallen barque-shaped oleander leaves.

COSTA DEL SOL: AFTERNOON

A light breeze blows the lavender blue
clusters of the jacaranda
tree, and a *bota*
cures in the sun on the balcony
rail. On the white hooded flue
of the German neighbor's house, three
white doves perch, stones. The red
bota sash winds twice around the nodule

of the molded granite head,
gun-slung: the *bota* is half full
of sun-hot rum. *Siesta*
at Las Columnas. Even the lizards wait
near the aloe and the cactus
spines for later, mimicking us
watching the landscape
colors of afternoon things, that *fiesta*

the eye follows into the sun's rings.

NIGHT SWIMMING AT LAS COLUMNAS AFTER THE DRIVE FROM RONDA

The soft afternoon argument
zeros in again face down in the twilight
pool, the winding mountain descent
to the white towns with names
ending in O and A, the driver's game
of precipice and brake, to these dream
lights halfway down the sides
of the cliff: *El Burgo* at the bottom

of the oleander stream. Not the surface slights
of hands that gather and part
soft waters in the night
or the verbal stabs that bide the summer's
discontent; I mean that old visitant
from childhood afternoons who yammers
long into evening, slips
into our dreams, that genie with the Sunday dinner

sigh who broods and snickers at our solitary
self. Turning herself in, reminding
us. Now these bats finger down
to our heads in the exact dark, sensing
us, turning over the Ronda cliffs
and the great forms of fish in the gorge
barely rising on their turns.

THE LIZARD OF VILLA DEL CORAZON

spots rose lice in a wink, combing
the morning garden on her belly rounds: fast

feeder feigning drowse in the afternoon sun:
roaming
eyes without a twitch, tongue-

tied until the flick. She outlasts
dogs with her breakoff tail

in the mouth. She's over the rail
in the dead thistle leaves, growing

another Borgia gown to fling. Her toes
quickfinger the twilight wall easy as flowing

water. She holds dead still until the patio light goes
off: her blue-pearl spots string

lightly down the back
of her invisible neck.

GRANADA

Inside the walls of Boabdil
we stroll the ruins of the barracks maze,
leave leisure at the blood canal
in the beheading room, gaze

toward the Sierra's glacial streams
above this garden red, these cedar
shadows outside the doomed suitors'
room. We throw our pocket's *pesetas*

at the fountainhead again,
hold our touch in check, examine
water lily pads on our knees
beside the blazing pools. We peel

one white spear for its wistful
smell. The feel
of this petal keeps the mystery
of knowing and leaving close,

this Alhambra eyelid for the journey
back, and one last surmise.

AFTER TROUT FISHING IN THE RIO FRIO

These peach roses bow
in the six o'clock sun, thin-
necked and collar-slack in
the garden row. How

ambrosial a pose
(rainbow trout, gill-red
in the finger grip, dead
weight) for the photo's

fast take before our lying
in the garden sun. Picture
the stream below the olive hill, its mixture
of bamboo and alder green in the drying

field rushing under
our feet, our poking poles
and the grasshopper twitch over the hole's
surprise. A snake, flour

white, slides away again
from the pink rose rising, slamming
the air, fish-tailing in the stream's
last breath, calming

in our heavy hands: white
petal scales, soft to touch in the sunlight.

I CAN HEAR CHEERS FROM THE BULLRING FOR LINARES

What under the sun
were they doing in this courtyard
of Roman kings: rings of columns

gathered from a Marbella field, shards
of polished granite strewn like snails
just off the coast? Old, cold sails.

CHURCH BELLS

Only the oleander blows
in the wind of this Roman
villa; an hour ago
William tip-toed a tarantula

on a white paper sheet
to the garden beyond the hedge:
Don't move baby, his feet
barely touching the crab

grass, and served it to the aloe
and the dust. Rose heads
float in the fountain pool. Now
they are trying to fly a round

kite with streamers, and give
it up. Today my father
will die again and row the river
home the twenty-seventh time

as the open summer looms
in Spain, clear as on that day
the Romans left these white columns
strewn in a Marbella

field. These daisies faced
the sun on the summer grass; this
white butterfly laced
the imperceptible breeze jumpgliding

the aloe and the fallen lemon leaves.

REMEMBERING THE NIGHTS AFTER THE OPERATION

From this distance, the mountain quarry
cleans the sky to a white blue
above the porcelain town; tomorrow

the first day of summer, that old clue
returning bits and pieces of the sleeping clown's
hat, bougainvillea over his knee

dreaming his broken hip in the rue
patch. The Spanish angel
wrestles him to the break of dawn

even in his dream, white bundles
over the first dark turning over,
as near as Jacob in the first light of summer.

THE SKY CLEARS ON SAN SALVADOR DAY

and the church bell rings afternoon
calm: the bullfight
begins. Over the mountain the moon
half-crowns the crest on its rough

side, granite scar to granite
scar under the sun. One
pipefish cloud drifts east. A mile
from the ring a man plays with a naked baby

in an emerald pool. The Mediterranean
is blue. Small boats make white
wakes. We have come to
begin. Our bread is a white

rose garden barely moving
in the breeze. In the bullring
Linares holds the *muleta* like a dove,
holding it in one hand, then the other.

THE SWALLOWS SWOOP OVER THE POOL

on the holiday of San Salvador:
trumpetings, the slow clearing
of the sky over last night's charcoal
grill, my old hip

calm in the courtyard of ceramic
pots, elephant ears
knitting. The shiny bone town
notches in the mountainside:

the afternoon of Linares and Galan
before the young bull yarns
unravel.

OVERCAST

The house binoculars close in
on our coastal castle there on the Marbella
road where nothing
stirs: our summer game of ruin,

ruin, for the album's page,
the slow unfolding of our childhood
play: our daydream days in woods
behind the row of poplars and the great

boulder where we could see
Winthrop Beach and Egg Rock so early
one morning we heard Mahan's cock
crowing. Here we

can hear only the lip-hiss
of the sprinkler in its periscope rounds
beneath the jacaranda tree, and the silence
of Spanish pines dead-still on the precipice

of our mountain's granite
gorge. Staying is nowhere
we knew even then, but being here
in the long view, simplifies, bit by bit.

WHITE DANDELIONS

White walls, white lace
over the Mediterranean, dark faces
from the old war, those ties
that bound us. Once we watched ghosts

in a yellow field. Here
the mayor hid for forty years.
The sun spots the busses gearing down,
the long climb to the white town,

the yellow eyes gone
white. Our blue eyes find
white bone.

TOLEDO: YOU POINT TO A STORK CIRCLING

a parapet and a nest of sticks:
My god it's a stork!

At the escarpment
you remember a dream: you
were very young, there
was a hatch of red moths
by a mill. Then you caught a great brown
fish. Then it was dying.
You were lying down.

On the bus to Madrid
there were fields of sunflowers,
and you couldn't tell, yet.

MADRID: SITTING FOR HER PORTRAIT IN THE PLAZA MAYOR

she forgets the rose's eye
closing in her pile-braided hair, the ivory
needle in her folded hands, her birthrib
scar under her marriage bib

and she breathes imperceptibly
near the beggar steps under the balcony
lights, remembering a child lost
in the finding of keeper's rules, the cost

of beauty's white thorn
and the picador's loss. No form
of accuracy can pin this down,
neither the artist's wit nor the bull's quick horn.

PAMPLONA, 8 A.M.: THE FIRST CANNON

booms. Caves open in the narrow
light, black bulls lift
up the harrowing
hill, skies of horn drifting

over their skull-white
eyes. Crazed white ducks criss-cross
under the steers' tight
turns: leghorns mass

rushing by the scaffolding
seams. A single hull rakes
doorways clean: dropcloths fold
under the thorn's quick stakes.

Estafeta Street bleeds
into the bullring. The second cannon
booms toward our afternoon needs:
the bulls will come one by one.

THE IRON BALCONIES ABOVE THE RUNNING BULLS

The stewardess from her crowded perch
over Estafeta Street brushes
her hair before the first bull rushes
the corner turn. The high-low game

tears through the hoof and cobble canyon
of the morning brain. Her vermillion nightgown
gashes the stucco walls, her dark brown
hair is down. The running bulls

are gone. Such high places
stay in the mind, these brushes
of death with our eyes: low bulrushes
zeroing in: fields of poppies blown.

THE BULL ENTERS THE BULLRING

shouldering the red wing blackbird
through the afternoon haze
of light, eye to eye, the pink blaze
THERE, blackthighs thundering back

to back *THERE*. He rushes the ringlight
prancing the gone field, horn-
harrowing the spiderform
neither here nor there over the sunbright

sand. The horns, god knows,
of his dilemma, are one
death in the afternoon sun: one
double dying inside the ring's repose.

"BEHOLD, THERE WAS A SWARM OF BEES IN THE BODY OF THE LION, AND HONEY"

The fishhooks swarm
in the bull withers hive;
honeycomb survive. Bull
blood is warm.

The matador kneels
between the double bulleyes;
he mocks the bull's
double dying. The matador heals

the bloodbright gashes
in the black neck dropping, rising
over the hooking horns, rising
over afternoon. Everything passes.

The sword-spear feels
through the honeycomb hive;
honeybrain revive. Bull
blood congeals.

SITTNG IN THE BULLRING

she fans and the cavalcade
of gold begins: the ballet of lady slippers
and May-apple tights: brocades
of leaves. She fans the sun
to the side of her face

and leaves flutter
to the sand. Her hand moves
in a deliberate stutter. She leaves
the bull to the pear-bummed picador's
foil and the ladybug's wing. She leaves

her seat without moving, remembering
sun-webs in a barley field and a hatch
of blood flying. The bull in a crow's remembering
enters the eye's silk sieve. Death
has all colors. There is

no ladybug and no bullring.

SITTING OUTSIDE THE TCHOXO BAR

her eyes sew the morning's
side. Circling the white
glaze, she follows the bobbing
gash of the torn runner's

dream, the giant heads nodding
no thighs for the king, no sash
for the matador circling
the blackbird's red wing: threading

the passion of San Fermin. Gypsy
bride: the red darning needle
wings at her neck fluttering.

ESPLA KILLS RECIBIENDO

and the sword hilt moves
slowly over the wet sand: the bull
grazes the sparkling corn moving
eyes the red cloths, full

circles the bees, oh honeycomb
cloth, homing in the strung
lights, the red foam
of the bees gone, mouth of the full lung

wet, of the heavy horns
the dark eye forms
the sailing of the bees
the lovely river soft the red red trees.

PAQUIRRI: POZOBLANCO

The butterfly fixes on the bull's red
sash: no sleight of hand
can stay his folded
wings above the darkening sand.

The butterfly stitches Spain's red
wound: sewing the lance-
cut with silver thread:
weaving red and red in the afternoon dance.

Everyone is running to the flailing
wings: breast pinned
to the blackened air, stick legs trailing
the shouldering snare. There is no wind.

26 September 1984

JOSE CUBERO, EL YIYO

and the horn raises from the withers eye
soundless, the bullring
upsidedown, hook and eye
of the needle eye threading

the yellow child sewn
in silk. The bullhorn
is mute, racking the thrown
silk doll torn

in one final gesture of stampede:
sewn with his own sword, mandrake
roots entwined: bleeding.
The bull dies for his own sake.

1964-1985

IT BEGINS AGAIN WITH THE BEES MUMURING OF THE SELF

in the Spanish poppy fields
beyond the summer train:
the window stain
in the photograph shields

them, but her neck burns
from the bee swarm
in the bull's withers, warm
with blood: she turns

each frame in the light
of fall, the yellow-red
cast of the girlchild's dread:
pumpkin loaves over the bullfighter

dead. The bees roar
on. Jose Cubero, El Yiyo
is dead. Thy banderillero's
rod and thy picador's

staff cannot comfort
him. *The bull has killed
me* is all
he said. The poppies sort

it out in the blazing
fields: capes
spinning: shapes
of bulls, grazing.

AFTER PAMPLONA: SHE RIDES THE BUS FROM
MADRID TO LISBON

with a fever, watching the fields
of sunflowers slowly turning
their heads, feeling

the white seeds blacken
in the heat. The bus
is relentless. Her skull

burns. That hull
of horns stopping dead again
on the turn, headhunting

the blind zone, streetscreams,
the red sash curling
the pool on his seedwhite thigh.

IN THE GARDEN OF THE CASTILLO

the gray nude statue
casts aside her downward
glance, and fixes her drawn

space so inevitably
inside her innermost place
that the words *chance,*

virtue, form
and *grace* fall from her
obedient shoulders

and weightless arms, to signify
the hollyhocks' vermillion
throats, and their wanton

yellow tongues.

SHE SWIMS ALONE IN THE MORNING POOL

and carries with the doe the stone
wall under her thighs
to the tapestry turn

as her body turns
itself at the end, feet
pushing off in one motion

into the underground pond
of feeder streams, star
rise, bottom light, her

overhand crawl in the morning
dream; cupping
hands into the mind's

ease, she releases
underneath the hind's
woven gains, the water

change, counts
laps, somersaulting at each
end, caping

with a sister dolphin
head down at the turn, belly
free in the water sun. Far

away, the hind
pursues the doe into other
rooms of the mind. Here

she swims alone, adding
unto herself and her long nasturtium
body, the easeful lane

of the miraculous pool.

and the orangutan slips
his mawkish, spitting rage
beneath the page
her hand stays, and she labors

the words *child*
and *friend* in mid-July
the way the butterfly
bemuses one, then another

oleander blazing among a thousand
quintuplets of lavender
words, lavender
repetitions she too slips from

into this summer
cage. Her folded knee
encloses her book, her free
hand, and she stays

until the last line
frees her. She sits
quietly until the cage fits,
and the lioness's moat disappears.

OUTSIDE THE CASTILLO, REMEMBERING PAMPLONA

the black swans
drift in the castlewater
ring, reptilian, quietly
stabbing the death
dream. A woman

reaches across queendoms
bread in hand; they castle
languidly in their dark
chess, and feed. A black bull
dies in her hands.

DOZING IN HOSTAL BURGUETE AFTER WALKING TO RONCESVALLES

I dream of Robert Lowell lost
down a well in a beech forest
dripping foxglove in a mist

beyond a turn, Roland's horn
sounding in the wind.
Already the foxes have the hind.

I try to save the thistles
in his heels (this blood rust
shutter banging, those split-tail

hawks above the field). Christ
knows this is a double story.
This was a Basque ambush party.

Today high above the pass
we found a beech grove with green blanket grass
by a communications tower, and higher

followed black iridescent sheep dung
beetles up the trail. On the rung
of the top ridge, a dark oak grove hung,

and grazing black-faced sheep
and horses moving in wind-deep
mist. I picked a piece of quartz for a keep

sake, and wildflowers, and headed face
down past the dove blinds and empty casings
scattered in the wet sedge erasing

each step to the pass, and the pilgrim trail
by the stream and the oaks to *Roncesvalles*
through the deep pink bells

of foxglove ringing. Can our pilgrimage be over?
At the feet of the iron oaks, in pockets of moss,
lie soft handkerchiefs of thousands of clovers.

EVERY DAY WE KNOW MORE EXACTLY

where we stand as the winds turn
spring inside out in late May:
tobacco fields brown the air with churning
earth, buttercups weave hay

fields where dandelions gave
up their ghosts weeks ago. We
know the earth holds us, grave-
standing as each petal waves goodbye

and we stand stock still in the garden.
Maple wings softpedal themselves to the black
earth. Every day we know when
the phone almost rings and we stand back

from the edge of the deck to make
sure in the dark, and our knowing
grows on the Stillwater Bridge where we take
our first spring communion of honeysuckle blowing

on the night wind. We know
where to step into the orchard
as the hawk raids, how
to stand still as the wind blows like a sword.

OCTOBER: DESCENDING HAWKS ROAD MOUNTAIN

tints of yellow in high apple
laurel on the trail's
brow
the pink cottony memory
of teaberry

taste this

III

"All the while you know that the muses, or the gods—call them what you will—are whispering to you. They cannot whisper words, for muses and divinities do not think in words, so they make sounds . . . ."

— *Joseph Brodsky*

About ending they were never wrong,
the Greek tragedians: how well they understood
the human entanglements that work
the final stage; how gods and goddesses shift
and shape the world, giving and taking
the dearest things; how family bonds are strange
and true; how passion punishes,
and creates the way.
They never forgot how enticing malice is,
how double-edged its sword, how the players
test justice and twist ends, how goodness
is in design.

Take Euripides' *Andromache* for instance,
where the players mingle the blood of Greece
and Troy, where dead Hector, dead
Achilles define the future carnal act,
where the human cast shadows itself in plot,
plays out our human days,
and sub-divides the end: Neoptolemus
(Achilles' son) dead at Delphi (at Orestes' hands);
his wife Hermione (Helen's daughter) run off
with Orestes (Clytemnestra's killer son); his concubine
Andromache (Hector's wife) off to Molossia
(to marry Helenus); Peleus (Achilles' father)
tapped for eternal life with the Sea-Goddess Thetis
(Achilles' mother),
where at the final exit the chorus
of Phthian women say:

A goddess clears the way for the unexpected.
This is how it always ends.

— *for Robert Bagg* —

DOMINO I, PARDONED BY CURRO RIVERA, SEED BULL AT LA GANADERIA CORTINA PIZARRO

in the days of the sun: *armada*
at noon, sails down
in the harbor of the hills. He moves

from our van in a manacled ease,
his loaves of testicles
bundling from his thighs, the old wound

heavy in his healed flesh, drawn
against these eternal hills
under this blue sky, and our flesh

healing from his, and from our own *cornada*.

AFTER THE TIENTA AT CHINAMPAS

Water hyacinths whitesilver the Rancho shore,
pardoned by the sun. Across the brown
lake I can see laundry
drying on bushes, a white heron.

Something says pay attention to cactus,
unpicked flowers, the small crimson
bird that flies from the grass
to the low limb of the *fresno* tree.

These hyacinths bleed
purple, shading into light.
Up in the hills, the lance cuts in the cows' backs
are earth red, healing.

SILHOUETTE

The opal ribbon above the ridge at dusk
narrows the last sky
from this kitchen window high
above the lake, below the oak tusks

black against the purple-blue,
a pure November view
of afternoon turning night,
color changing hue,

as the other ridge from the other dark
weighs down its eyelid stone.
Now true west itself is gone.
Now dark against dark, and the inner view.

ARMISTICE DAY, LAKE WYNONAH

the way the brown fields fold down
the ravines
and the furthest ridge lines
blue over the nearer oaks and pines

the way a small dark bird emerges
from a branch hold
eye level
in the backyard pine and urges

beaksfull of cavity-black from the trunk
leaning slightly
from the stiff-backed masthead oaks
above the lake

the way November brings its truce
and the oak leaves shuttle
yard to yard toward the subtle
corners of our lives, parchment

piles that return time
for sweeping clean
the way the lake awakens in November
to a bluer blue and a deeper line.

ASSISI AND PERUGIA

Below Mount Subasio
Saint Francis sleeps underneath his Brother Snow;
his green bones double-cross
his single-bedded crypt. Lying low
he settles our loss,
we who walk upstairs to Giotto.

Outside, the gift
shop keeps our scrutiny dear; we lift
gilt-edged porcelain bowls in bird
design, buy a white Assisi blouse, shift
our gaze again to the street stirred
into frenzy by the snow beginning to drift.

Our Fiat spins up the cobbled hill
to our exit square, and the snow squall
stops as if cast by a pilgrim's
spell. White roads lace the Spoleto Valley
along its olive rims
as the small towns hold us: Spello,

Collepino; then our midnight walk
through the Etruscan gate to the Rocca
Paolina: the escalator's stages
inside the Perugian walls. The talk
of Francis from this lookout rim is ages
old: Brother Relic, that hawk-

faced boy who kissed
the leper on the lips: humorist
of birdsong and the Gospel's wit: simplicity's
son who changed hands with Christ
in the world's loveliest complicity
of tone. This glow from Assisi insists

on a candle's power, shadowlight
and the soft touch of time: acolyte
of the Umbrian hills. The dark
surrounds this spring night
from all sides. We mark
time here on these Etruscan heights.

turns the sunflowers down
beneath the weed witch's broom
and the cicadas' drone.

The blue stalks mourn
in their garden room,
beat from the summer sun,

full of it. Halo drawn,
they overshadow the corn.
Two miles away the Etruscan

tomb opened under the farmer
ploughing his field and the loam
turned bright below the mountain

haze in an instant's change of tone:
Umbria opening
on the original plan.

Not even La Fontaine
could turn the cicada's tune
to a wastrel's use of time.

Now the witch's broom sweeps clean
this blue Tiberian afternoon
in monochrome, and the sun

pours down
its yellow rain.
Drenched heads hang like Raggedy Anns.

WALKING FACE DOWN GIACOMO PASS, FORMAZZA, AFTER DRYING IN THE REFUGIO MARIA LOUISA,

the gentian violets quicken the fog
slope; surefooting, we print the grasshoof
cheek down the gigantic view. the soft bog
of the herd's grazing, shifting the roof
of tones lower to our left. In the white
plastic bag, our wild lake trout sags
in the curve of his last fighting

leap from *Lago Castel*. He is rag-
limp, firm, the gold faded
from his stomach white, his black spots
ebony in the lowering light. Our shepherd's
paths keep ending. Caught
again in the deepening July rain,
(hooded) we imagine ourselves down the quilt
of this dark alpine terrain.

A RIVERBOAT ON THE LUJIANG

after dark in mid-July in Guilin:
black cormorants glisten
in gas lantern light on the thin
bamboo raft beside us. They hustle off the stern
and on, off the bow and on

fishing for their keep,
coughing it up. There is a child asleep

in the stern. In the dark I cannot imagine
the sunlight water "green and crystalline"
and autumn banks "bright with golden
persimmons, pomeloes, and tangerines." The lantern

light plays on birds sleek as stoats,
on their rigged throats

beyond our bow. We can almost touch them.
Now the child in pajamas leans
back asleep in her mother's lap. The captain
is her father. He signals the fisherman
we've had enough. The light goes out and we head in.

XI'AN: THE UNDERGROUND TERRA COTTA WARRIORS
OF EMPEROR QIN SHI HUANG (221 B. C.)

stand in the trenches of a government
dig. The smell inside the pavilion
is university cage with a dirt floor
in summer. Light pours down
through the glass roof on the regiments
of the Qin Dynasty's guard, four

after four to eight thousand. Above the first
pit we lean on the guard
rail and overlook the coiled hair
coiffures and the open fists
grasping air where the spears disappeared
in the infantrymen's hands. Charioteers

have lost their reins. They seem to concentrate
on what lies ahead. They have been lying down
for two thousand years, broken at the waist, strewn
in their battle robes and plate
armor tunics among bronze arrowheads with chromium
tips. Some have defended the Emperor's mausoleum

with their heads on a comrade's neck
in a touching affectionate burial reversal of the law
of harmonious form. Now they stand by
the thousands, risen under the restorer's eye
with brush and glue, and we stand on this upper deck
in a soft brown light in awe

of these sunken corridors of thousands of different Chinese
mustached faces and the stillness
of this army's motion below our own sculpted faces.
We leave to search for two bronze chariots
and horses with bridles of gold facing west
below Li Mountain and the orchards of apricot trees.

THE BLUE WATER BUFFALO IN THE CAVE PAINTING
IN GUANGXI

stands facing me, his backside
to the wall in a thicket of brown
dreams. His thin horns
spiral over his blue oiled hide

in spindly vertical curls, old hat,
primal sheen. The blue buffalo
dreams himself. His fat
form frames a blue glow

where the light shines. Outside, China
glows in another light. The sky of Guangxi
tones down the pinnacles from an ancient sea.
In my own dream cave I'm back against the wall.

New blue buffaloes eye me still.

REED FLUTE CAVE, GUILIN

Under Guangming Mountain we idle
barefoot at the lighted limestone pool
at the turn of the horseshoe cave. Pearl
drops of limewater seep silently into the shallow

miniature lake. On the walls
shadows come and go as passers screen the pastel
glare reflecting off the bone facades of parables.
They point and stare: an ivory traveler

on a plateau ascends above a frieze
of fawns, white broccoli trees,
boulders of brains. Pearl crawly bees
investigate. "When the Japanese

bombed Guilin, 30,000 people waited here." Now the primal
waters stir with bathing feet. Grandmothers dangle
babies, dip them laughing. These cool

cauliflower columns melt outside in the July
heat. Silent melodies of reeds play
over the lake. Bamboo raftsmen steer lovers on holiday.

AFTER THE EVENING MEAL WITH JIANG HUA'S
FAMILY IN SHANGHAI

Jiang Hua escorts us up the bamboo
ladders to the open window and the view
of rooftops brushstroked on the sky. A sheen
of blue oil darkens over the summer East

China Sea. We can almost touch the painted gashes
across the alleyway. The single slash
of a red support cane deepens the blue
frame of a neighbor's bedroom window:

Jiang Hua says the government wishes
to tear down all the private houses
in our view. Our view is personal. Below
on the Chang Ning Road, watermelons pile

the curbstones where we walked and bargained
two hours ago. Now we walk again
into the long file of sycamores, black
overhead, the hollow sounds

of patted melons offered from the dark
Shanghai night, ripe, heavy, almost perfectly round.

PIANOS AND TEMPLES

In early morning drowse I dream an old friend
from Swan's Island, dead seven years,
brings Paderewski's heart to my childhood kitchen
on Cleveland Avenue for my mother

to wash for the burial. I show
him how I jury-rig my jigsaw blade
to make do. "Here's the heart," he says,
tossing a paper box on the table.

No one plays the piano in the other
room. It is like after the deer
Uncle Harry shot, and how he brought
the funnies on Wednesday night. The box is square.

My mother has no qualms. When I awake
a purple finch is sitting on the feeder
outside the window, his splashed breast
glistening, the first

one I have seen all winter. It is the second
day of spring. Now I am in
the sunken living room reading
5 A.M. in Beijing. A robin

flutters and claws at my bow window
beyond the China bowl
with blue osmanthus blossoms and butterflies
and the kerosene lamp with the glass flue

ruby in the sun, and the five bass flies
on the sill that Arnie Sabatelli tied
for me at Christmas, two yellow and three
black, as the poems tie China

line by line out of my hands. Wen Song
and Xiao Zhen, that evening near the Xiamen
campus when the sun blazed on us by the lotus
pond and we couldn't see the water

beneath the pads, still radiates all the colors
in China's black hair, and the way we sat
back from the edge, from the heartbeat
of the heat itself, and made small talk

about the great gun that haunches
above the beach near the new white building
shaped like a piano. A song
plays silently over the lotus pond,

and then our bodies walk
to dinner. In dreams the dead talk
straight to the heart. It is more than art.
It is the best part

of ourselves.

YOU CAME UP FROM THE TIDE POOL

with a pocketful of periwinkles
that Sunday morning in August
before the wind shifted east
and the blown petrels laced the darkening
waves: sprinkles first,

then a higher sea watermarking
the seawall beach, then larch arms
drunken across the window sky. At night
the waning moon lighted
the punky walkway from the car,

and the tentative deer
crossed silently toward the shore.

A WHITE SAILBOAT IN LATE JULY

slides soundlessly behind the west Sister point
as the grasshopper touches down and sailflutters up
and settles on our deck. His ladyfinger flaps
grind his own ax in the summer sun:

relax. I watch his tucked wings mimic
the rotting bleached-cracked spruce
until he jumps the southwest breeze. Summer arithmetic
in yellow blotches scars the blueberry sea.

THE LOBSTERMAN OFF RED POINT

hauls his string of summer traps, and the buoys
line the sealess morning calm. Offshore
the whistler's ten second moan sounds another
story. Across the deck a small boy

learns addition and subtraction in Chinese. Later
he will make a drip castle on Fine Sand Beach
as the tide goes out. But now the morning's summer
eases into color and sound, teaching

the calculus of tone. Yellow jackets
prowl the railing spruce. Overhead a plane brackets
the blue sky looking for herring. You read in the sun,
your long black hair pony-tailed for fun.

THE SHOALS BETWEEN RED POINT AND THE SISTER

islands whiten the mid-channel
darkline:
foreground poplar coins

rattle the fog flannel
sky. Add
wild roses and the lost gold mine

near Black Point.
My view
is chartless, blue

across the water's sheen. The shoals,
fifteen feet
down, anchorpoint

the sailless sailboat's dream.

MID-TIDE: FAMILIES OF BLACK DUCKS

dabble in the rockweed rising
and lowering in gentle swells:
soft

squabble across the water, emphasizing
summer calm. Below, brown bales
of kelp

unravel. When the ducks beeline
for the rainbow pots
beyond

the ledge, heart green
poplar dots
enlarge

the puzzle's theme. Nearby
you teach a small boy words
in late July.

DUCK HUNTING WITH KAIMEI AT THE OTTER PONDS

When the two Goldeneyes took off at the far end
of the first pond, they headed West,
then turned and came for the quarter moon
behind me, bright white in the late November

afternoon, rising like sixty over the blue stone
beach under my feet, gunning the best
flap they could muster, already at max duck
speed, the drake flying co-pilot six feet

behind, although I confirmed that only with luck
later, after I leaped the low tide channel
to the rock island haired with kelp, and picked
him from the soft lee of the deep water side

belly up, moon white in a small funnel
cave, rising and lowering in the soft lap
of the incoming tide. There was a small
red spot on one breast and a broken

wing. When I handed him over, Kaimei
handed me back my gun. The hen
was re-crossing overhead in the first of three
passes. "Did you hear me yell?" she

asked. "I couldn't see you from the end of the beach."
We watched the hen land ocean side, beyond gun's reach.

WALKING TO THE "INDIAN CAMP"

something about a meadow soaking wet with rain
in late October, and the golden
leaves, about coming around a bend
above a thin creek, and Indian names,
something about the Indians
gone, a logging road running back into the hills,
about new turnips broken
and scuffed in the trial, something
about a great earth mound
at the clearing where shanties fell down
and yellow leaves blazing in the rain
something about not dying
and dying
something about yellow leaves and names
where an Indian girl had lain
something about a yellow wood
on a Sunday in the October rain

THE WHITE DEER

Looking out my upstairs study window at four
o'clock, combing the white woods beyond my white
deck as far as the stone wall, even a few yards more
into the pines, along the slim maples to the white

swamp and the dirt road, I imagine a deer browsing head
down in the snow. His black nose roots under his rack.
He is pure white, feeding, following the stone wall. I read
of it once, one in several million, the albino buck.

Such visions persist in December. This one turns brown
and is gone. I hear a shot beyond my neighbor's home,
then another, and I count five. Someone shooting his own
dream, I muse. I turn to my poem, my father still down

in the autumn well, and hear a final shot. He's done in
now, at last. A line of shots is a running deer, but one
alone is the fatal wound, the one that blasts the mirage.
Three weeks now, my doe has been hanging in the garage.

JEU DE BOULE AT SUNSET: BIMINI

in a high January wind, the absinthe sea
black milk: palming the gray steel suns
above the slamming surf: listen
to the pelicans, glideblown, silently

foray the palm-torn air, dropping
and rising, now wind-swept above the beach
in double silhouette beyond our reach.
Only the sounds of the waves and the plopping

ball settling and rolling in the terrace
sand define this hour before the amyrillis sun
descends the rim—then the green
flash—and dark. We leave these measured spaces

by the edge of the Queen's Highway
to walk the night calm near Poggy Bay.

PARADISE BEACH

A pelican fishes the school of jacks
sparkling the unruffled tide,
working her glide-dive-glide
over the whitegreen bay. Nothing distracts

her from her amiable concentration
on the underwater zircon flash
repeating down the white curving sash
of beach. Back beyond the opal mansion

on North point, offshore, they say an ancient roadway
lines the ocean floor, grand chiselled slabs of stone or reef
arranged for a quarter mile, they say
perhaps a lost civilization come to grief,

perhaps New Atlantis, here, right under our feet.
The wind blows up and we body-surf the waves.
Lying in the sun we watch the sand crabs leave their caves.
The pelican fishes by. Our eyes do not meet.

ON THE BALCONY OF THE COMPLEAT ANGLER

The bougainvillea petals on the vacant tennis court
deepen the whiteness of the hanging shark
in the sunset southwest breeze, the white northern yacht
porcupine in dock,

white knives glistening in the smiling snarl
upside down, white bullion in the dream cruise
suspended, the bougainvillea coral
on the brain vine; now the white bruise

glides again in the channel tide beneath
our drifting afternoon boat, "There,"
you said and it is gone into the dark teeth
waters of our minds, out there and in here.

THREE DAY BLOW

The names of fish watercolor the whitecapped
waters of Poggy Bay;
call it January mindplay
when the palm crowns lean and the torn buoys map

the shore. Only the eagle ray
clowns in the channel stream
washing himself clean
of suckers and flukes, gray

against the aqua velva of the churning bay.
Gone are the strawberry groupers, cotton wicks,
yellowtails, gone the blue boxfish with hornpricks,
the queen triggerfish grinding their molars, you say,

for the devil of it. The ray
baptizes himself in the empty waters of the flannel
air, leaping from his channel
lair. The fish hang outside for another day.

BONEFISHING

A great white heron looms
in our binocular oval frame
on the low tide flats, slow motion
picky, his sandbar

barely under water: milkfeather
white in the afternoon
sun. Here on shore
grave piles of conch shells,

sunset red, labial,
the conch divers gone
for the day. Terns
play on the wind, crying. I

remember yesterday, Cordell
poling on the flats, spying
our steel white bonefish. Dry,
the scales are tough as thumbnails.

WHITECAP FOAM

bunches on the high tide beach
of Poggy Bay, the sixth day
of our January blow. Sponge size pieces
roll across the ivory sand. You say,

"Look at the terns on the sandbar
with their lovely orange beaks."
Later, their sentinel line breaks
as they fly, and little cries from far

away seem all around us in the wind.
Little foam piles blow across my mind.

FISHING THE FULL MOON

The concrete wall of the Big Game Club
shadows our dangling legs before the tide
turns, and the barracuda silvering on its moon side
drifts from the late docking yacht,

heading for itself further on. We rub
shoulders, bait casting in the dark, our caught
snappers flopping now and then in the plastic
grocery bag, our lines slack and taut

in the channel rush between the coral grass.
Our seasonal harbor glistens in our bridal
dark, our shark white moon rides its tidal
mark. Our fingers listen for the barbed hook's grasp.

When Bonefish Rudy killed the motor in the shallows
of the mangrove swamp in Bimini Bay
we could see a narrow winding way
through the bowlegged maze, a natural cut to allow,

at least temporarily, a journeyman in
to the fresh mineral springs said to ease
the body and restore the soul, even to tease
the doubter to behold its baptismal gin.

In this case, a journeywoman. When Rudy said
we'd have to walk it from there, I knew
I was safe, and she would never walk through
the mangroves, barefoot, but I was dead

wrong. Without a word she slipped off her shoes,
slid off the bow and headed in, a turn
on the old childhood game even she had learned
in the other world, and I couldn't even choose,

whether I was ready or not. So I followed behind
as she picked her calf-deep pace. The bottom was firm,
and we steadied on the solid vines, worming
our way. Overhead, the gray clouds were lined

with black, and the wind came out of the West.
Our little boy was waiting with Rudy in the boat,
relieved not to be commandeered. We could have floated
in the pool by swinging out to its deepest

level by a rope looped through a high mangrove limb,
but one quest was enough. A faint mineral scent
was in the air. With whatever else was there, it meant
something. Kaimei was satisfied. We edged along the rim

of the Healing Hole and picked our way back
to the boat, ready to go bonefishing,
though the sky was now black.

CASTLES, 4:00 A.M.

Listening in the dark to the storm
surf and the wind rustles
of the window blind,
I remember today's castles

on the beach, how we trenched
the draining moats on our knees
before each ninth wave drenched
the job, collapsing

the pearly shell roads
ascending the spiral rims,
each fistfull a truckload,
building Troy ten times,

Herculaneum even,
even Lhasa, my stepson Chen
so happy to begin again,
so happy in the sun

feeling his solid knees
before the vanishing cities
of a morning's play, dispelling
that old saw about dwellings

and sand, here on Atlantis
where the mute egrit stalks,
where the frantic gull screeches,
and sharks feed off calm night beaches.

— *for Yunwei* —